KAISER colour

# magical mist

COLOURING BOOK

40 whimsical designs

KAISERCRAFT



Kaisercraft Pty Ltd.
2 Bayldon Crt, Breakwater
3219, Victoria
Australia
www.kaisercraft.com.au

First printed in April 2018

ISBN; 978 - 1 - 925405 - 65 - 1

Proudly Printed in Australia

All illustrations featured in the book are original.

THIS BOOK BELONGS TO

..............................................................................................................................

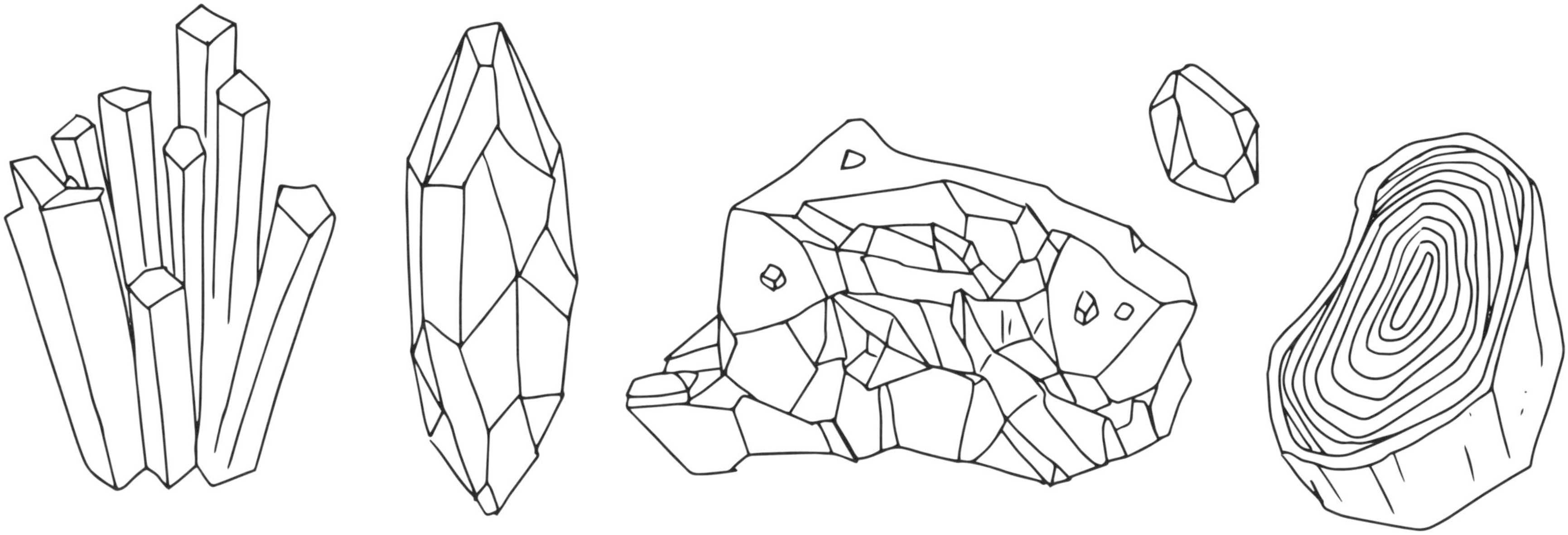

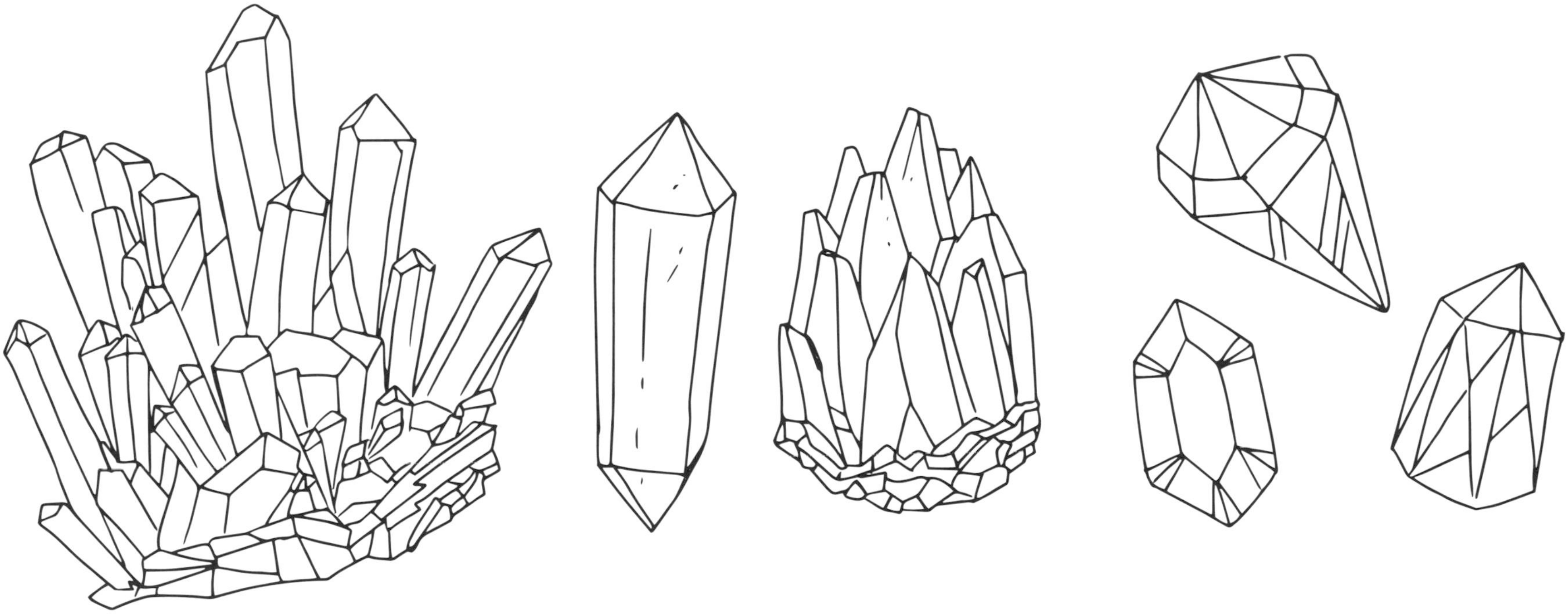

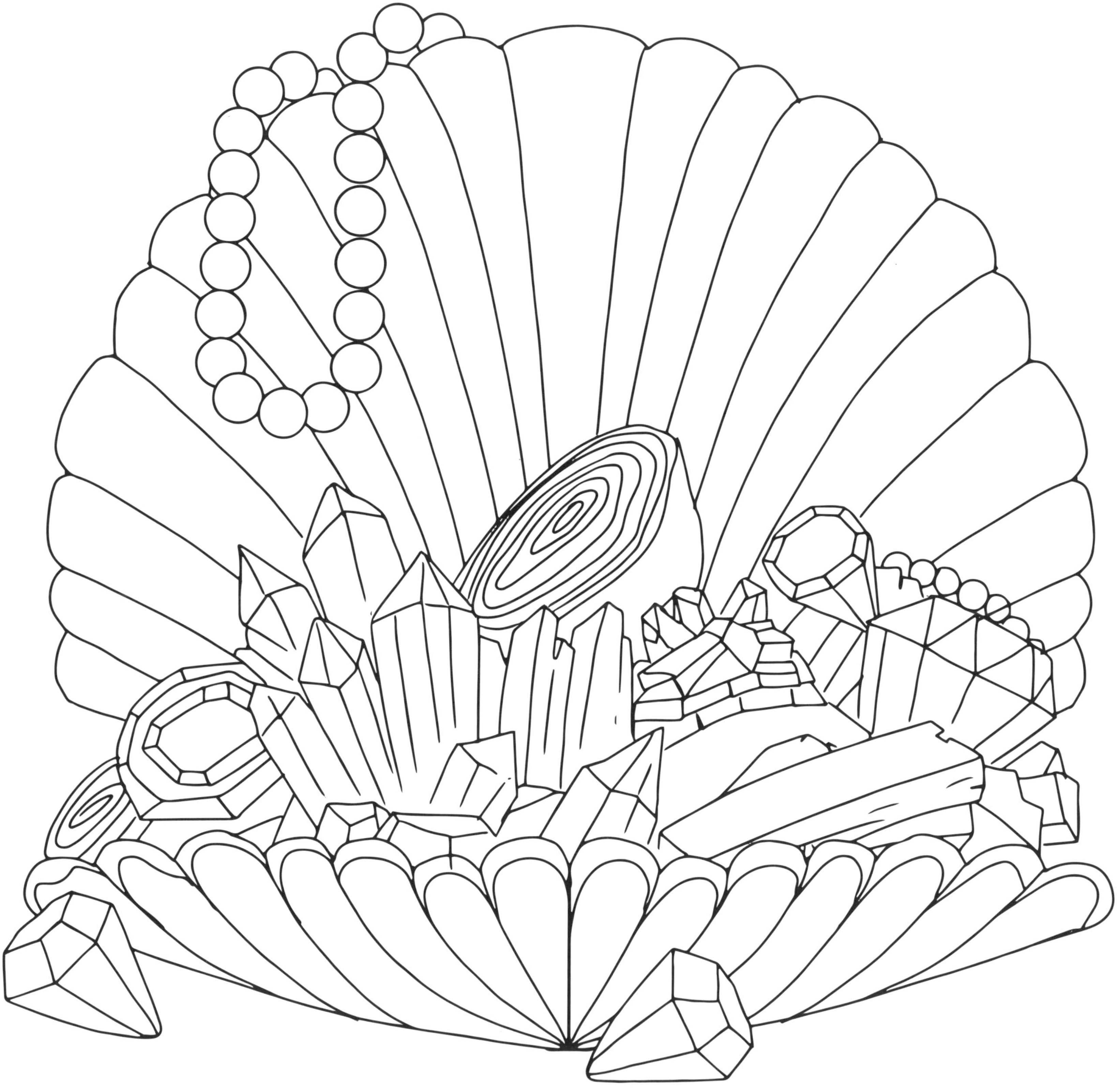